# Psychic Development Exercises and Techniques

Charles Mage

Published by Charles Mage, 2023.

While every precaution has been taken in the preparation of this book, the publisher assumes no responsibility for errors or omissions, or for damages resulting from the use of the information contained herein.

PSYCHIC DEVELOPMENT EXERCISES AND TECHNIQUES

**First edition. May 27, 2023.**



ISBN: 979-8215529638

Written by Charles Mage.

# Also by Charles Mage

Magickal Imagination: Learn to Use Your Imagination in a
Magickal and Witchy Way
Dowsing the Casino: Make Money Dowsing
Magickal Partnership
Energy Ball Manual
Sex Magick for the Solitary Practitioner
Elemental Invocation
Vampirism Magick for Beginners
Vril Mastery: Harness the Force of the Gods
Psi Constructs
The Magickal Mindset
Instant Magick for Everyday Use
Healing with Psi
Magick as a Way of Life
Dowsing Without Tools
Learn to Create an Astral Temple
Fun Things to Do with Your Energy Ball
In Search of Beauty
Imagination Magick: Learn to Use Your Imagination to Live a
Magickal Life
Pendulum Magick: Communicate with Spirits
Magick in Your Pocket: Magical Spells You Can Cast
Anywhere, Even in Your Pocket!

Make Your Own Magick Wand The Intuitive Way
The Way of the Magus
The Secret Occult Techniques of Making and Using a Ouija
Board
Mistakes and Pitfalls in Magical Practice
The Magick of the Zenina Circle
Escape Life with Your Imagination
Experiments with Magical Energy
Elemental Magick of the Five Fingers
Magical Keys to Self-Empowerment
How to Acquire & Take Care of Magickal Creatures
Beat the Casino Using Clairvoyance
The Magical Art of Mental Projection
Mindcraft Spells Starter Manual
The Magick of the Holy Rosary
How the Rosary Changed My Life and How It Can Change
Yours Too
True Initiation into the Craft of Magick
The Way of the Pendulum
The Christian Magician
Shamanic Journey for Beginners
Life Lessons from a Butterfly
Psychokinesis Manual to Beat the Casino and Make Money
Phone Sex Magick
The Magick of Writing
Energy Servitor Manual
My Magickal Rosary Journey
How to Create an Elemental Servitor
Basic Wizardry 101
Create an Alter Ego for Work Success and Peace of Mind
Finding Christ in the Occult

Psychic Development Exercises and Techniques

Watch for more at https://www.czlibrary.com/.

# Table of Contents

*For Cris & All True Practitioners of the Craft Magickal...*

# Introduction

*Psychic Development Exercises and Techniques* is a manual that teaches how you can awaken and develop your psychic abilities. Psychic power is not just for those who are gifted, but it is for everyone. Every human being is blessed with psychic power. However, you need to awaken and develop this power for you to be able to use it. Although it is true that some people are naturally gifted with active psychic power, it does not mean that you cannot awaken your inner power. Indeed, it has long been established in psychic and occult communities that we all have the ability to harness our magical power, and the potential that we can reach is infinite.

*Psychic Development Exercises and Techniques* lays down the foundation and gives practical exercises and techniques to awaken and develop your psychic power. True psychic power is not something that you simply believe in, but you must experience it actually and personally. This book provides the training that you need to undergo to awaken the power that lies within you. Whether you are a complete beginner or an intermediate practitioner who is looking for a way to immerse yourself in the magical world, then this is the manual for you.

Psychic power is a general term that refers to various kinds of magical powers and abilities that you can exercise. Nevertheless, every psychic training that you engage in will develop your overall psychic abilities and skills. As such, no training is ever wasted. The good news is that developing your psychic power is not difficult; however, the question here is if you are willing to dedicate the time and effort to actually train your psychic senses.

Never think that you are not good enough to awaken your psychic power. You must realize that the power that you seek is already within you; it is just a matter of letting it out. This manual is more than a set of theories and instructions, but it is an invitation to a wonderful and magical journey that might just change your life forever. I have also included exercises and techniques that I have learned from the occult and psychic workshops that I have attended. I hope that this humble work would serve as a guiding light to help you find your own path and actually experience the beauty and power of true magic.

# Understanding Psychic Power

To understand what psychic power really is, we have to look at the main word: psi. Psi means energy. All things in the universe are made of energy. Psychic power refers to the power to harness and manipulate this energy in order to create the change that you desire. It is important to emphasize that the power that you seek is already within yourself, and that you do not need to look further away. The more that you seek outside of yourself, the more that you will get lost and not find what you are looking for. But, if you learn to look within yourself with stillness of mind and heart, you might just be surprised with the beauty and wonder that you already possess.

Once you awaken the psychic power that lies within you, you will be able to do various things that most people can only dream of. You will be able to heal diseases using psychic means, move objects with your mind, levitate, see and communicate with spirits and various magical beings, and even protect yourself and others from negative energies and psychic attacks, among others.

The world of psychism is actually a huge universe, and you may want to choose which parts of this universe you would like to specialize in. Do not worry if you do not know yet at this point what captures your passion; you will realize this as you make progress on your magical journey.

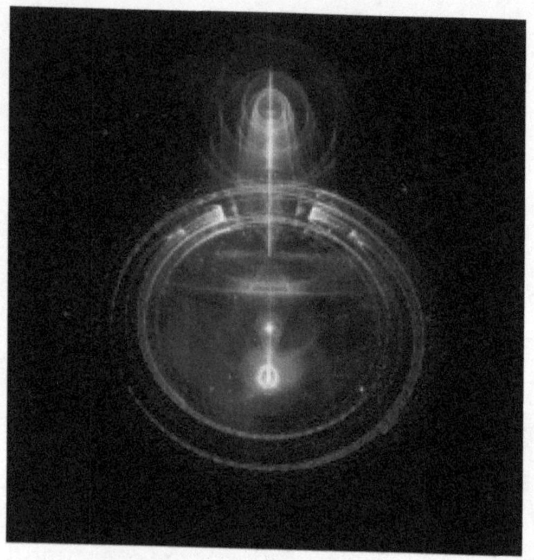

There are many people who now consider the realm of psychism as a form of science. Although the abilities that you can exercise once you awaken your psychic power may look like a miracle, this is only because most people do not understand the forces that are at play. But, in the eyes of someone who has psychic training and knowledge, it is only normal and expected for you to be able to do magical things once you awaken the power within you.

Psychic power is not a new thing; it has been in existence since the beginning of time. However, the modern world has changed the ways of man, even how we think and feel. If you want to awaken your psychic power, then you must free yourself from the many illusions and trickery of the modern world. In order to awaken your psychic power which lies within you, then you must not look elsewhere but within—and this leads us to our next subject: meditation.

# Meditation

When it comes to awakening your psychic power, perhaps there is nothing that could be more important than the regular practice of meditation. Meditation is a way to connect with your soul, as well as to free yourself from the many illusions of this world. Meditation will still and calm your mind, then it will also develop your overall psychic skills and abilities.

Psychic power is already present within you. Technically speaking, it is not even asleep, and so you do not even need to wake it up. The problem is that it is often shrouded by so much noise and worldly thoughts and worries, so much so that it could not manifest itself before you. If only you can still your mind even for a minute, and you will realize that you truly hold divine power. This is where meditation comes in, and meditation will allow you to fully realize your full potential, as well as the power to harness the forces of nature.

As for your first practical exercise, you will engage in meditation. The meditation technique that you are about to learn is an ancient practice. I first learned about this meditation when I attended a Buddhist meditation seminar. This meditation will also allow you to have a glimpse of the magical dimension. This meditation is known as the inner light meditation because it uses the innate and divine light that is always present within you as the point of focus of the meditation. To help you better understand what this meditation is all about, let us discuss the actual procedure:

Assume a comfortable position and relax. Close your eyes and do nothing about anything. You must understand that the time for meditation is not the time to think and analyze things; but rather, it is the time for you to become still and experience the beauty of pure being. If thoughts surface on the mind while you meditate, even if the thoughts appear important and reasonable for you to think about them, you must ignore them during the meditation. Do not worry, you can think about whatever concerns you may have after the meditation.

With your eyes closed, consider everything that you see that is not black as light. This is your inner light, and it is the light that always shines even in darkness. It is also believed that this inner life is always connected to the Divine Light, Who is the Creator of all things, visible and invisible.

Now, gently focus on this inner light. Do not try to understand or analyze it; but rather, just be with it and let go of everything else. Allow the inner light to guide you and take you forever you may need to be. There is nothing that you must do but to let go of everything, including yourself.

As you make some progress on this meditation, you may start to see images and visions unfolding right before you. You do not have control over what images or visions you may see and experience; but do not be afraid because you are being guided by your inner light—and it is the light that overcomes the darkness.

Simply observe and enjoy the magic unfolding right before you. This is the magic of the universe revealing itself to you. Do not even attempt to understand or analyze what is happening. Activating your logical mind will only prevent you from going deep into meditation. Again, the time to think is after the meditation session, but never during the actual meditation itself. For now, just relax and enjoy.

You have a free choice to end this meditation at any time that you want. To do this, simply recall to mind your physical body and return to it with the act of your willpower. Once you can sense your physical body again, slowly move your fingers and toes, and very gently open your eyes.

After awakening from meditation, think about the experience that you have just had. You might also want to write it down in a notebook so that you can have a clear record of your meditation journey. Now is the right time for you to think and analyze the experience. Still, do not forget that it is not advisable to rely so much on your logical mind because the logical mind is very limited in scope and ability. In fact, many practitioners of psychism and the occult see the logical mind as something irrelevant when it comes to dealing with matters of the soul and magic. Instead, you must rely on your heart and your intuition.

The practice of meditation is very important if you are serious about having any real positive progress on your magical journey. In many of the occult and mystery schools, it is recommended that one should meditate at least twice daily. Take note that this is only the minimum requirement; and therefore, if you can do more, then by all means do so because it would be very beneficial for you.

# The Power of the Mind

The key to awakening and using your psychic power lies in the mind. The mind holds the power of the imagination and thought, which are the key ingredients in developing and exercising your psychic power. If you want to activate your psychic power, then you must take good care of your mind. When it comes to taking care of the mind, once again, the practice of meditation is highly desirable. From now on, you must also be careful with the thoughts that you keep and entertain in your mind. You must only fill your mind with positive thoughts and get rid of all negative thoughts as quickly as possible. Never forget that your mind is your most important and powerful weapon, and this is true both in the realms of psychism and the occult.

But why is the mind so important? It is with your mind that you will be able to harness the forces within you and all around. It is with your mind that you can manipulate energy and use it to manifest your desire. If you are wondering how can the mind be able to do all these things, then the reason for this is that your mind is always connected to the Great Mind, The Creator and Origin of All Things, Visible and Invisible. Since you are always connected to the Ultimate Source, everything is possible.

Although every human being has a mind, only a few know how to use the mind psychically. This is the big difference between a layperson who does not know anything about psychism and someone who is educated and trained in the way of the true psychic. A psychic must have good control over their own thoughts and be able to direct them in a magical way. In our world, so many people are controlled by their thoughts and emotions instead of the other way around. We are in an ocean of energy; and if we are not careful enough, we can easily be bombarded with and even manipulated by the energies of others, thereby causing us to lose sight of who we really are.

The mind can be our friend, but it can also be our worst enemy, depending on how we deal with it. To awaken and make use of your psychic power, you must learn to master your own mind—because when you do, miracles will naturally unfold in your everyday life.

# Bubble Shield

The bubble shield is one of the most basic psychic shields. It is also very effective, which is why so many practitioners of magic love to use it. The power of this shield depends on the skills of the one who casts it, and so it simply gets more powerful the more that you develop your skills. Casting the bubble shield requires that you tap and harness psi energy, which necessarily includes exercising your psychic power. To help you better understand the creation of the bubble shield, let us discuss the actual steps for its creation:

Be comfortable and relax. You may close your eyes, if you want. Imagine psi energy all around you. You are free to visualize it in any way that you want. It is usually recommended to imagine psi as being made of pure white light. Still, you are free to visualize it in any way that you want. The important thing here is that you must know in your mind that it is psi that you are imagining. Now, once you can clearly visualize this psi all around you, see and feel that you are drawing it toward you, and then have it form into a bubble all around you. This is your bubble shield. Know that this shield protects you from all harm, negative energies, and psychic attacks. However, this shield is still weak; the next step is to empower your shield to make it strong and effective.

Continue to visualize psi all around you. See and feel that you are continuously pulling this psi toward you and pour it into your psychic shield, thereby making your bubble shield more powerful. Keep adding more energy into your bubble shield until you are satisfied with its power. You will know if your bubble shield has a good amount and level of energy because it will light up and shine in your mind's eye. This is a common sign of a strong accumulation of psi/energy.

Once your bubble shield is set, you can further impress its function by saying a magical affirmation, such as the following, "This is my bubble shield, and this bubble shield protects me from all psychic attacks and negative energies." In line with the universal rules on affirmations, be sure to craft your statement of affirmation in the present tense, and be sure to believe in whatever it is that you are affirming.

When you engage in the world of psychism and magic, it is important to learn how you can defend yourself from psychic attacks and negative energies. It is noteworthy that there are many kinds of beings in the universe, and some of them are drawn to humans who practice the craft of magic. It is also worth noting that the world is now full of negative energies, and it is good to protect yourself from the illusions and vain influences of the modern world.

On average, a bubble shield should last for about five hours, but its life can be increased depending on the skills of the magus and how much it is exposed to negative energies. Do not worry, if ever you do not feel it anymore, you are always free to make a new one. After all, the bubble shield is one of the psychic shields that you can safely cast as often as you want and as many times as you want. Just give this shield a try and see how it works for you.

# The Infamous Psi Ball

The psi ball is one of my most favorite psychic exercises and techniques. The practice of making a psi ball has significantly developed my skills in the direct and active manipulation of psi. It has also developed my overall psychic skills and abilities. As such, it is definitely one of my most favorite practices. What is a psi ball? As the name already implies, a psi ball is a ball that is made of pure psi (energy). To create a psi ball, all that you need to do is to accumulate and concentrate psi into a ball.

A psi ball has various uses and applications. You can do whatever you want with it. You can play with it, throw it at an object or even on the wall, and you can also throw it at someone to catch their attention, and so on. A psi ball can also be used for healing. Having said that, let us now discuss the actual steps:

Be comfortable and relax. Clear your mind and do not think about anything. Position your hands in front of you as if you were holding a ball, palms facing each other. You are going to accumulate psi between your hands, and that is where your psi ball is going to be.

Imagine energy all around you. Again, white light is recommended, but you are free to visualize it in any way that you want. See and feel that you are drawing this energy toward you and have it form into a ball between your hands. Keep adding and accumulating psi between your hands. As you do this, see and feel your psi ball getting stronger and stronger. You should be able to see it lighting up in your mind's eye. This is your psi ball, and you are free to do with it as you please.

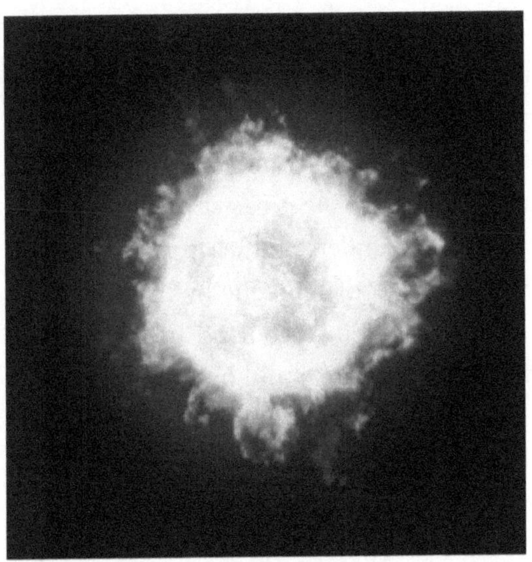

But how do you know if you have truly created a psi ball and not just imagining things? There are certain signs to know that a psi ball has, indeed, been created by a magus. The signs may vary but usually appear in the form of warmth in the hands, pressure, heat, and/or a tingling sensation. It is also possible to see the space where your psi ball is located to look blurry in the physical plane. This blurry vision is usually due to the high concentration of psi in one specific area.

You can make your psi ball look like anything you like. The important thing is to know in your mind that it is your psi ball. In the spiritual world, appearances alone do not matter that much since they can be changed almost instantly with just the pure effort and will of the mind. Do not worry so much about how a certain thing looks, but be more aware of how they make you feel. Now is the time for you to train yourself to trust in your intuition and open your heart.

So, once you have made a psi ball, what can you do with it? For starters, it is good to play with it, such as by passing it from hand to hand. You can also throw it at a wall and catch it as it comes back to you. The purpose of this game is to get used to your psi ball, as well as be able to better understand what psi is all about. You can also catch the attention of someone by throwing your psi ball at them. Do not worry; since your psi ball is made of energy, it will not hurt them, but it should be enough to catch their attention and make them look your way. This technique is also known as pinging, and it is as simple as throwing your psi ball at someone to make them take notice and look at you. It is good to practice this technique in a public place. Simply choose a target, throw your psi ball at them, and then see what happens. It is also worth noting that you can easily make a psi ball with your hands under a table—this is a helpful tip when you want to make a psi ball in public without being noticed. In fact, once you get used to the process of making a psi ball, you will not even have to use your hands anymore. You can simply imagine psi gathering at a specific spot/area and forming into a ball. Still, if you are a beginner, using your hands can be very helpful, and it will also allow you to be able to feel the presence of your psi ball being created.

If you want to use your psi ball for healing, simply imagine the energy of your psi ball as being made of pure healing force. You can then use this energy to heal yourself and others. Simply place the psi ball at the area that requires healing, and see as it unfolds its magic of healing. Last but not least, you can also move physical objects with a psi ball by throwing the psi ball at the object. It is suggested to experiment with light objects in the beginning, such as a balloon or the flame of the candle. You can then increase the size and weight of the object as you gain more experience. There is so much to say about psi balls since they are highly versatile and reliable. Feel free to use them in any way that will please you. With a ball that is made of pure psi, there are simply so many wonders and possibilities available to you. Open your mind and let the magic ignite.

# Psi Healing

Are you interested in using your psychic power for healing? Psychic power can be effectively used to heal yourself and others. In fact, there are special courses and practices in psychism that specialize in healing. A good example of this is pranic healing, which is the magical art of healing using prana (another name for psi) alone. Hence, it can also be called as psi healing.

Psi healing is holistic. This means that it heals at all levels, which is actually the best way to heal. This is different from the way conventional science heals where it only heals the symptoms, but not the main root cause of a dis-ease. Psi healing is also free. You can learn to do it and use it to heal yourself and other people, and even animals and plants. In fact, places can be healed, too. The truth is that everyone deserves to be healed, especially considering the fact that the world is now a very difficult place to be in. There is simply so much negative energy going around, and it is very easy to be influenced by negativity.

The good news is that psi healing is not difficult. It is a psychic ability that you can easily learn and use. After all, the universe is also full of psi force energy, and it is just up to you to tap onto this force and use it for your healing purposes. To help you understand how this works, let us discuss the steps:

Be comfortable and relaxed. Clear your mind and do not think about anything. Close your eyes and let go of everything. Once you are feeling still and calm, imagine a brilliant ray of light descending from heaven, and see and feel the ray of white light entering your body through the crown of your head. Know that this ray of light from heaven is made of pure psi of healing. It heals everything that it touches.

As soon as the ray of light touches and enters your head, you should be able to feel its healing force. Allow this healing light to fill you gradually from head to toe. As it passes and spreads all over your body, feel it healing every part of you. Continue to draw more and more healing energy through the ray of light until you are completely filled and overflowing with healing force. You should be able to see yourself shining brightly as you are filled with healing energy.

Once you are done, you can conclude the exercise by visualizing the ray of light slowly fading away, but be sure to keep all the healing energy that you have already absorbed within yourself. You can then go about your day while full of healing energy.

Know that this healing psi shall continue to heal you as long as it remains with you.

Instead of absorbing energy through the crown of your head, you can also accumulate healing psi between your hands. Simply imagine psi energy all around you—again, seeing it as white light is recommended. You can then draw this psi and pull it between your hands as if you were making a psi ball; however, this time, know that it is not just raw psi that you are manipulating but that the psi is made of pure healing force. It is that psi that heals, and it heals thoroughly and powerfully. You can then use your healing psi ball to heal anything that you want. All that you need to do is to send or place the healing psi ball in the area that needs healing.

The ray of healing light can also be directed to another person instead of yourself. The steps are the same except that you should see and visualize the ray of light healing another person instead of yourself. This means seeing the ray of light descending and entering the crown of the head of the person whom you wish to heal. From here, simply allow the ray of healing light to fill and heal them from head to toe. If the person whom you want to heal is not physically with you, you can imagine them right in front of you, and you are free to do with this imagined figure whatever you want to do to the actual person, knowing in full faith that this imagined figure is a magical representation of the actual subject, and that whatever is done to this magical representation is also done to the actual subject. This is not just a trick of the imagination, but it takes advantage of the power of the imagination and the fact of spiritual connectedness of life and all of creation.

# Touch the Earth

To touch the earth means more than touching it physically; but more importantly, you ought to feel the connection—because this is how you touch it with your soul. Since you came into this world, you have always been swimming in the rich green energy of the earth, and it is the energy that nourishes and heals you. Especially in this modern world, it is very easy to get lost in this world, and so we need to find our roots every now and then.

The technique that you are about to learn is considered a basic technique in witchcraft, with a modification that uses the hands instead of the feet. This is to better emphasize actually touching the earth. Here are the steps:

Relax. Place your hands on the floor, palms touching the ground. Feel the earth beneath you, and feel your connection to Mother Earth. Next, imagine roots like those of a tree slowly coming out from your hands, and send these roots down into Mother Earth. Allow the roots to go as far as they want to go until they stop naturally. Now, hold this position and appreciate your new and more intimate connection with the earth. Many times, having this deeper connection with the earth is enough to make you feel better. But, you can still take this technique further by absorbing the fresh green energy of the earth. To do this, inhale—and as you inhale, see and feel that you are absorbing the earth's energy through your roots, into your hands, and into your body and being. Let every inhalation be a way to absorb the energy of the earth into yourself. Continue until you are satisfied with the power that you have absorbed or until you are filled and overflowing with the earth's fresh healing energy.

When you are done, thank Mother Earth for her help. You can then pull your roots back into your hand or simply visualize them slowly fading away. You can then go about your day knowing that you are now charged with the energy of the earth.

# Psi Push Method

The psi push method is a technique that is used in telekinesis. It is a way to move an object with your mind by pushing it with psi. You can also apply the same technique on humans, and it usually has the effect of drawing their attention to you or even making them move in accordance with the direction of how you push them through psychic means. Still, it is most common to use this psychic technique on objects as a way to train yourself to harness psi, as well as a training for the feat of telekinesis. Having said that, the steps are as follows:

For this exercise, it is good to use a light object, preferably a balloon or the flame of a candle. If you are using a balloon, place it on a flat and smooth surface. You are going to accumulate psi, and then you will use that psi to push an object, thereby causing it to move physically. Choose either hand. You can use either your left or right hand. I even know some practitioners who like using both hands at once. Imagine psi all around you in the form of pure white light. Next, see and feel that you are drawing this white light toward you and have it accumulate in your hand. See and feel the white light energy pouring continuously into your hand, thereby making the psi accumulate in that hand.

Keep adding more and more psi into your hand. You should be able to feel the build up of psi in your chosen hand, and your hand should appear shining and glowing with psi in your mind's eye. Once you are satisfied with the accumulation of psi in your hand, it is now time to use it to push/move an object. Position your hand a few inches away from the object that you intend to move, palm facing the object. Now, see and feel that you are projecting the accumulated energy toward the object like a beam of light, thereby pushing it and making it move. Keep pushing it with energy until the object finally moves.

This technique usually takes practice, but it is also effective and very much worth learning. You can also apply the same technique on humans. The effect may vary from person to person, but its effect is undeniable. If you are looking for an interesting magical experiment, then this one should definitely be on top of your list.

# Levitation

The power of levitation is something that has been sought by various practitioners for a long time. Levitation defies gravity, and it is a feat that is undeniably amazing and unbelievable. But, how does one learn to levitate?

You must know that the power of levitation belongs to the air element. To levitate, you need to charge yourself with the power of air. You do not need to make your whole body levitate right away. The best approach is to do it gradually starting with just one finger. Here are the steps:

Place your hand on a flat surface. Gently focus on your pinky or index finger. Next, imagine air all around you. You may see the air as some kind of white-colored energy. Some people like to visualize it as a yellow-colored energy. The important thing here is to know in your mind that it is energy/psi that you are imagining.

Next, see and feel that you are drawing this energy and pour it into your finger. Keep charging the finger with the air element. As this happens, see and feel your finger getting lighter and lighter. If done correctly, soon enough, the finger concerned will rise/lift on its own without any physical effort or force on your part. This is the power of levitation as applied to a single finger. The next step is to use this technique to levitate your other fingers until you can levitate your whole hand and even your whole arm. After achieving gradual success, you can then charge your whole body with the air element and make yourself levitate. You can also charge other objects with the air element to make them levitate. The important key here is to be able to harness the power of the air element and direct it to fill and levitate whatever you charge with it. Here lies the secret of meditation, and it is only up to the practitioner to practice and master this ancient feat and magical craft.

# Spirit Sight and Communication

The technique that you are about to learn will allow you to see into the spirit world and even be able to communicate with the beings that belong to that plane. For starters, you must realize that you are not a stranger to the spirit world. This is because you are also a spirit. The body is yours, but it is not you. You are first and foremost a spirit. Therefore, do not think that seeing spirits is an unusual thing.

To see into the spirit world, you must learn to close your eyes and look with the eyes of the mind. Open your mind and stop logical thinking. Once you learn to see with the eyes of the mind, you will be able to experience the mystery and penetrate into the divine mysteries. Having said that, here is a technique that you can practice to see and communicate with spirits:

Be comfortable and relax. Close your eyes and clear your mind. While keeping your eyes closed, imagine the room where you are in. Look around you using the eye of the mind. Know that you are now looking through your magical eye. After all, your physical eyes are closed, so the only sense of sight that you have is the magical sight. Do not try to control what you see. Instead, just relax and keep an open mind.

The next step is to invite a spirit to make itself known to you. To do this, simply give a welcome invitation, such as by saying, "If there is any spirit around, I welcome you to make yourself known. With love and light, appear." Say this thrice and just wait for a spirit to surface, if there be any. If nothing appears, do not be discouraged. Just try it again some other time and also in some other place.

If you badly want to see and communicate with a spirit, know that you can always invite your spirit guide. A spirit guide is a spirit who has been guiding you in this life. To invite your spirit guide, simply call out to it. You can do this by saying, "My dear spirit guide, please make yourself known to me and appear." Feel free to use a different statement of invitation in accordance with your personal preferences.

Just wait for a spirit to appear in your imagination. Once a spirit appears, feel free to talk to it. Talking with a spirit is easy. We usually do it by telepathy, but you are also free to talk out loud, if you want. As you communicate, just be sure to keep your mind open so that you would know if the spirit is sending you a message.

# PSYCHIC DEVELOPMENT EXERCISES AND TECHNIQUES

It is worth noting that the physical world co-exist with the realm of the spirits. We all live in one universe, so do not think that they are far away from you. Moreover, do not forget that you are, first and foremost, a spirit. You are a spirit who simply has a physical human body, thereby allowing you to have a human experience. Still, the very core of who you are is a pure spirit.

# Dowsing

Dowsing is a psychic technique that is used in divination. Divination refers to magical techniques that allow you to look into the future, as well as a way to gain answers. There are various ways to do divination, and dowsing has been considered as one of the best methods of divination. Dowsing can also be made in various ways, but the most famous is with the use of a pendulum. A pendulum is commonly defined as any weighted object that is suspended on a string or thread. It is probably the most common tool that is used in dowsing.

You can purchase a ready-made pendulum from an occult store, but you can also make your own from simple items that you most probably already have in your home. If you are a beginner, it is recommended to simply make your own pendulum. All that you need is a thread and a needle. The length of the thread may vary, depending on your personal preference. The important thing is that it should be long enough to allow the bob to hang still and also be able to swing freely. Simply tie one end of the thread into the eye of the needle, and this will work just as any other pendulum. The needle will function as the bob of the pendulum, and the thread shall be as the chain of the pendulum. With enough practice, you can be an effective dowser even with a simple pendulum. After all, the pendulum is only a tool—and you are still the dowser.

To use a pendulum, you must first know how it answers. To do this, hold your pendulum by the thread and wait until the needle (bob) is hanging still. Once it is still, tell your pendulum, "Show me yes." Wait and watch out how the pendulum moves. The bob (needle) should swing in a particular direction and manner. Take note of this because this is how your pendulum moves to signify an affirmative answer. If the pendulum does not move, simply repeat the statement until it finally responds.

The next step is to know how your pendulum responds when giving a negative answer. To do this, simply tell your pendulum, "Show me no." Wait and take note of how it moves to signify a negative response. The movement should be different from how it moves to signify an affirmative answer. Once you have noted how your pendulum moves for a yes and for a no, then you are now ready to put it into actual use. Here are the steps:

Hold your pendulum by the thread and wait until the needle is hanging still. Now, ask your question. The question should be answerable by a yes or no only. Wait for the pendulum to respond. If the pendulum does not respond, just relax and repeat your question. For example, you can ask, "Is there a spirit in this room?" Feel free to ask your pendulum any question that you want. As long as it is answerable by yes or no, then you should be able to get a response from your pendulum.

Dowsing can be used for various purposes. It has been used to locate hidden treasures, find lost objects, know the gender of the baby that is still in the womb, identify diseases, communicate with spirits, and simply as a way to gain wisdom and insight, among others.

# Whirling the Aura Technique

Whirling the aura is a technique that functions as a form of psychic self-defense. It should be noted that the aura is already a natural form of psychic protection that we have. But, with the right knowledge and skill, you can significantly improve its protective power. One of the ways to increase the defensive power of the aura is by whirling it around yourself. This will make the aura more defensive by immediately deflecting any and all negative energies and psychic attacks that come in contact with it. I learned this technique from a Wiccan friend who, in turn, learned it from an energy healer. Fortunately, whirling the aura is easy to do. Here are the steps:

Stand and relax. Imagine your aura around you. Your aura is an energy field that surrounds your body. You can simply imagine it as white light around you. Feel free to use your intuition to visualize your aura. Now, move and turn your body slowly in a clockwise motion. In magic, clockwise is for casting, while counterclockwise is for banishing. As you turn your body clockwise, imagine that you are whirling your aura around yourself like a whirlwind. See and feel your aura turning and turning like a whirlwind and know that all negative energies and psychic attacks that come in contact with it shall be immediately deflected.

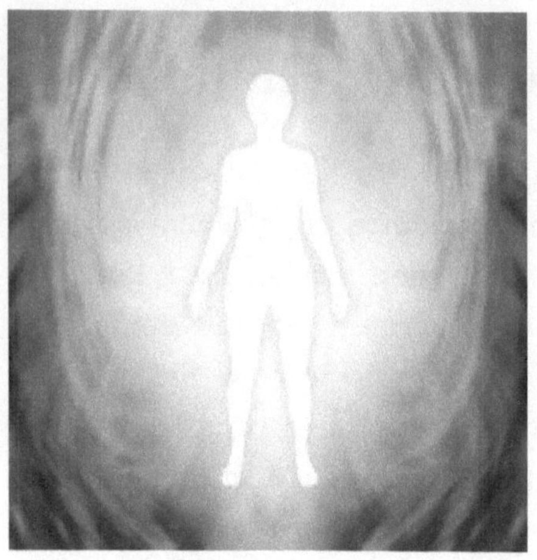

In the beginning, turning physically clockwise can be very helpful; but as you get used to this technique, you will soon be able to cast it even without physically moving your body. After all, it is a well-established teaching in the magical arts that all true and most genuine magic starts and ends in the mind.

By whirling your aura, you create a vacuum that deflects energy instantly as soon as contact is made. This is a really useful technique to use, especially when you know that you are being targeted by a psychic attack. This technique is also used in many witch wars. Another good thing about this technique is that its power is in accordance with universal rules. Even if the psychic attack is very powerful, it can still be deflected because the aura will confuse the energy of the psychic attack, causing it to disperse and become lost in the ether. Just give this technique a try and see how it works for you.

# Cleansing Breath Technique

The cleansing breath is a way of breathing that helps you release negative energies from your system. It is a technique that was developed in the practice of yoga, but its practice is also present in many of the occult and magical arts. It uses the breath as an aid in manipulating energy; and in the process, it results in the exhalation and complete release of negative energy from your body and soul. There are adept practitioners of this technique who are able to cleanse themselves of negative energies in just a single breath. Having said that, here are the steps:

Relax and do not think about anything. Inhale through your nose and exhale through your mouth. Now, take a deep breath—and as you exhale, see and feel that you are not only exhaling air; but that together with the air, you are also exhaling all the negative energies that you may have in your body and soul. You may visualize the negative energy as some kind of black or gray smoke. It does not matter how you visualize it as long as you know in your mind that it is negative energies that you are exhaling out of your system.

Let every exhalation be a cleansing breath. Continue breathing in this way until you feel that you have been thoroughly cleansed. With enough practice, you will soon reach a level of skill that you can cleanse yourself of negative energies with just a single breath. It is not really necessary for you to reach this kind of level, but it is nevertheless doable since many adepts are already using this technique in this advanced manner. Whenever you find yourself in a difficult situation and whenever you feel like you are being bombarded by negative thoughts and energies, feel free to use this psychic technique to cleanse yourself and get rid of negative energies.

You can also take this technique even a step further by absorbing positive psi from the universe. To do this, inhale—and as you inhale, imagine that you are breathing in pure white light. Know that this light is made of pure psi that is charged with pure love and kindness. Let every inhalation fill you with this divine energy. Hence, inhale positive psi and exhale negative psi. Continue this breathing cycle until you become completely cleansed of negative energies and charged with pure positive psi. Breath is life. If you master the breath, you can learn more about life and be able to use it in a magical way.

# Mirror Gazing

The practice of mirror gazing is an ancient practice, and it is also a very interesting technique especially if you are the type who wants to see something so clearly in front of you before you believe, in line with the saying, "to see is to believe." Mirror gazing is an exercise that will allow you to see various faces in the mirror. Although you may not have any control of the face that may appear, the effect is very clear and interesting that you might end up doing it so many times simply because it works wonders. For this exercise, you are going to need a simple mirror. It should be big enough to allow you to see your whole face. The steps are as follows:

Prepare a mirror and place it in front of you. Now, look at yourself in the mirror and just relax. Look at a specific point on your face and gently focus on it with a relaxed gaze. You should be looking at this one little point, and you should be aware of your peripheral vision. Just relax and let go. You will start to see some features of your face changing slowly. When this happens, just relax and do not change your focus. Continue to focus on that little spot and just look with your peripheral vision.

Allow any changes to unfold without trying to control it. You should soon be able to see a completely different face in the mirror with your peripheral vision. It may take some getting used to seeing with your peripheral vision, but you will surely get used to it easily. You will be guided by the new face that will appear in the mirror, which makes the use of the peripheral vision easier and much more fun.

In case nothing appears and you do not see anything, do not be discouraged. Just give it another try and never stop practicing. When you use this technique, it is important to relax and to keep the mind open. Do not force yourself to see anything. This kind of magic should happen smoothly and naturally without using any kind of force. Make use of your peripheral vision and get used to it. As you focus on a specific point, changes will occur in the background. Look at it using your peripheral vision as you keep an open mind.

# Auric Sight

Developing the auric sight is something that many practitioners of psychism and magic often want to gain. Once you gain the ability to see the aura, you will be able to gain more insights about the person who holds the aura. There are two ways of seeing the aura: physical and psychical.

To see the aura physically, you need to learn how to see with your peripheral vision. To do this, look at a specific point and stare at it with a relaxed gaze. You should soon be able to activate your peripheral sight. When this happens, allow your peripheral vision to show you whatever it is that you must see. During this moment, you must keep your mind open and do not judge or analyze anything. Using your logical mind usually tends to put an end to any magical experience. Hence, you should avoid thinking. Instead, you should immerse yourself in the magical experience by enjoying it; and as for thinking and analyzing what has happened, you can do that later on.

To see the aura of a person, look at their third eye, which is located right between the eyebrows. Fix your gaze at this point and then allow your gaze to relax. This will activate the peripheral vision. When this happens, do not force yourself to see anything. The more relaxed and open you are, the more easily that you can perceive the aura. You can also easily see your own aura by looking at your hands. Simply choose a finger and stare at the tip of this finger. Allow your gaze to relax to activate your peripheral vision. Just wait and see the aura as it becomes visible to you. It usually starts with a faint white light similar to a glowing light. This is the first level of the aura, also known as the etheric aura. With enough practice, other colors will also emerge.

The aura reflects your current magical and spiritual state. By learning to see the aura, you can see and gain more insights into people and things. You can also gauge your physical and spiritual health by learning about your aura. By seeing and reading the aura of others, you can also gain more insights about them, and you will also be able to understand them better. The aura is the emanation of the soul. It is a natural energy field, and there is so much that you can learn from them. If you want to gain more insights and be able to read a person like a book, you will do well by paying attention to their aura.

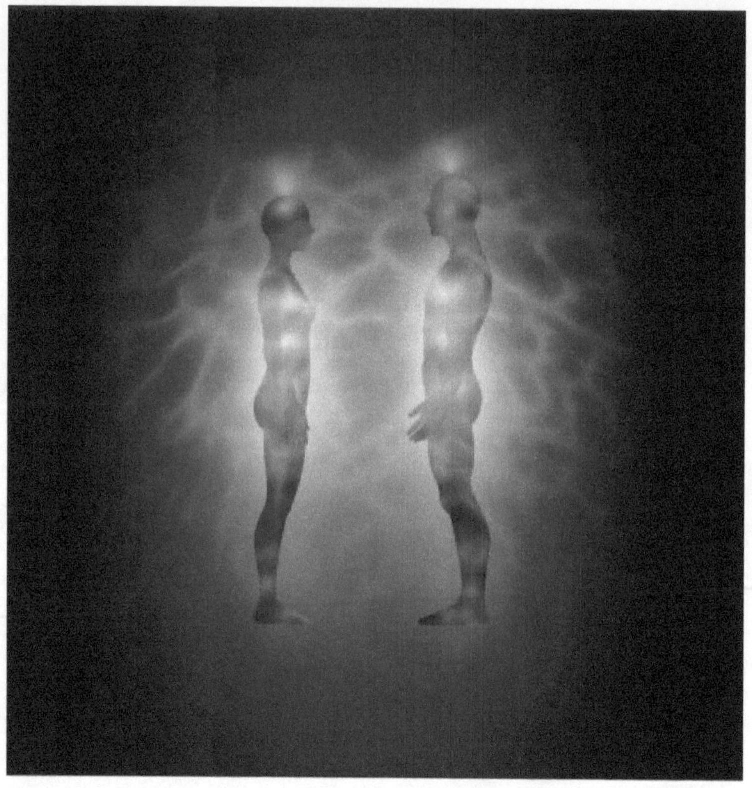

Seeing the aura through psychic means requires mind training. You need to learn to harness your imagination. You will not force yourself to see an aura, but you should learn to keep an unbiased and open mind. To see the aura psychically, you can close your eyes and imagine seeing your aura. Yes, this is a very direct approach that requires an open mind and reliance on your intuition and imagination. Just accept whatever you see as your aura. What color is it? What does it look like? The more relaxed you are, the more easily that you can perceive your aura with accuracy.

Of course, you are not limited to simply seeing your own aura. You can also see the aura of other people, and even the aura of trees, plants, and objects. After all, everything in the universe has an aura. Just give this a try and see how it works for you.

# Candle Flame Exercise

I learned this psychic exercise from a very dear and close witch friend. This exercise will significantly develop the power of clairvoyance, thereby allowing you to have a much more powerful imagination and be able to see with your mind much more clearly beyond time and space. It will also develop your overall psychic senses and skills. For this exercise, you are just going to use a candle. Place the candle either on the floor or on a table in front of you, and light it.

Relax and stare gently at the flame of the candle. It is ideal to do this exercise at night where the room is only illuminated by the flame of the candle, but any other time and place would also work just fine. Gently focus on the flame of the candle in exclusion of all other thoughts and ideas. If thoughts arise in the mind, gently ignore them. Only focus on the flame; the flame is light, and light is truth.

As you stare at the flame of the candle, soon enough, visions may begin to unfold in your inner sight. This is your clairvoyant power getting activated. When this happens, gently shift your focus to the visions. Do not force any vision to appear, but everything must happen naturally and smoothly. Surrender to the light and allow it to guide and take you wherever you need to be at this moment. Just relax and enjoy as the magic of the flame, which is the magic of the universe, unfolds right before you.

To end this exercise, slowly shift your awareness back to your physical body, move your fingers and toes, and gently snap out of the meditation by returning to normal consciousness.

# A Message

I hope that you have enjoyed our magical journey together. The best way to awaken your psychic power and to use it regularly. Not only will this awaken your psychic power, but it will also develop and make it more effective and powerful. Never forget that you already have the power that you seek within yourself. You are naturally psychic and magical. You just have to realize it by letting the power out of you. Of course, the way to do this is through continuous practice.

It should also be noted that the practice of psychism is an art. As such, feel free to make adjustments and developments to the techniques and exercises in this book in accordance with your personal preferences. In fact, you are even encouraged to come up with your own ideas and techniques. After all, the craft of psychism (and magick) is a constantly evolving science and art. We must always keep on learning and doing our best.

By awakening your psychic power, you will have various powers and capabilities at your disposal. How you use these powers will be under your full control and responsibility. It is asked that you use the knowledge that you gain from this book only for good and good alone. Never forget that whatever power or magic that you cast, it shall always find its way to you sooner or later. There is an energy link that connects us to everything, including all the magic that we do. We must also not forget that the true practice of psychism is primarily a spiritual pursuit. Therefore, it should help make us become a better human being with a soul that is overflowing with love and kindness.

Last but not least, enjoy every step of the journey. After all, this journey has no end. May you find the meaning and the reason behind the great power that you possess, and may you wield this power with love always in the fullness of your heart. I wish you all the best on your magical journey.

# Don't miss out!

Visit the website below and you can sign up to receive emails whenever Charles Mage publishes a new book. There's no charge and no obligation.

https://books2read.com/r/B-A-SXMH-WIQJC

Did you love *Psychic Development Exercises and Techniques*? Then you should read *Energy Ball Manual*[1] by Charles Mage!

*Energy Ball Manual* is a magickal manual that will teach you the ancient science and art of creating a powerful energy ball. Indeed, creating an energy ball is of great interest to a magickal practitioner that it is only right that a whole occult manual be written about it.

*Energy Ball Manual* is divided into 4 parts:

Part I talks about the theory behind the creation of an energy ball. Before you create an energy ball, you first need to be equipped with the right knowledge behind this magickal feat.

---

1. https://books2read.com/u/31xEQr

2. https://books2read.com/u/31xEQr

Part II discusses the actual steps on how you can create an energy ball. Be sure to read the instructions carefully and study this how-to guide. Do not worry, I have written it in a way that is simple and easy to understand.

Part III shares important tips and pieces of advice that you should observe to further increase your chances of success.

Part IV gives answers to frequently asked questions regarding the creation of an energy ball.

*Blessed be!*

Read more at https://www.czlibrary.com/.

# Also by Charles Mage

Magickal Imagination: Learn to Use Your Imagination in a Magickal and Witchy Way
Dowsing the Casino: Make Money Dowsing
Magickal Partnership
Energy Ball Manual
Sex Magick for the Solitary Practitioner
Elemental Invocation
Vampirism Magick for Beginners
Vril Mastery: Harness the Force of the Gods
Psi Constructs
The Magickal Mindset
Instant Magick for Everyday Use
Healing with Psi
Magick as a Way of Life
Dowsing Without Tools
Learn to Create an Astral Temple
Fun Things to Do with Your Energy Ball
In Search of Beauty
Imagination Magick: Learn to Use Your Imagination to Live a Magickal Life
Pendulum Magick: Communicate with Spirits
Magick in Your Pocket: Magical Spells You Can Cast Anywhere, Even in Your Pocket!

Make Your Own Magick Wand The Intuitive Way
The Way of the Magus
The Secret Occult Techniques of Making and Using a Ouija
Board
Mistakes and Pitfalls in Magical Practice
The Magick of the Zenina Circle
Escape Life with Your Imagination
Experiments with Magical Energy
Elemental Magick of the Five Fingers
Magical Keys to Self-Empowerment
How to Acquire & Take Care of Magickal Creatures
Beat the Casino Using Clairvoyance
The Magical Art of Mental Projection
Mindcraft Spells Starter Manual
The Magick of the Holy Rosary
How the Rosary Changed My Life and How It Can Change
Yours Too
True Initiation into the Craft of Magick
The Way of the Pendulum
The Christian Magician
Shamanic Journey for Beginners
Life Lessons from a Butterfly
Psychokinesis Manual to Beat the Casino and Make Money
Phone Sex Magick
The Magick of Writing
Energy Servitor Manual
My Magickal Rosary Journey
How to Create an Elemental Servitor
Basic Wizardry 101
Create an Alter Ego for Work Success and Peace of Mind
Finding Christ in the Occult

Psychic Development Exercises and Techniques

Watch for more at https://www.czlibrary.com/.